We're Going to the Smiths' House

A Book about Apostrophes

WHITING PUBLIC LIBRARY
1735 OLIVER STREET
WHITING, IN 46394

by Marie Powell
illustrated by Anthony Lewis

amicus readers
3

Say Hello to Amicus Readers.

You'll find our helpful dog, Amicus, chasing a ball—to let you know the reading level of a book.

1 Learn to Read

Frequent repetition, high frequency words, and close photo-text matches introduce familiar topics and provide support for brand new readers.

2 Read Independently

Some repetition is mixed with varied sentence structures and a select amount of new vocabulary words are introduced with text and photo support.

3 Read to Know More

Interesting facts and engaging art and photos give fluent readers fun books both for reading practice and to learn about new topics.

Amicus Readers are published by Amicus
P.O. Box 1329, Mankato, MN 56002
www.amicuspublishing.us

Illustrations by Anthony Lewis

Produced for Amicus by The Peterson Publishing Company and Red Line Editorial.

Editor Jenna Gleisner
Designer Jake Nordby

Printed in Malaysia
10 9 8 7 6 5 4 3 2 1

Library of Congress Cataloging-in-Publication Data
Powell, Marie, 1958-
  We're going to the Smiths' house : a book about apostrophes / by Marie Powell ; Illustrations by Anthony Lewis.
    pages cm. -- (Punctuation Station)
  Mya and Tyson search for their friend's house and help each other learn how to correctly use apostrophes in a sentence.
  ISBN 978-1-60753-729-8 (library binding)
  ISBN 978-1-60753-833-2 (ebook)
  1. English language--Punctuation--Juvenile literature. 2. Apostrophes--Juvenile literature. I. Title. II. Title: Book about apostrophes.
  PE1450.P68 2015
  428.1'3--dc23
                                    2014045807

Punctuation marks help us understand writing. Apostrophes show when something belongs to someone. They also take the place of letters when two words join together to make a shorter word.

Today we're going to Paul Smith's house.

On their way to the Smiths' house, Mya sees wet paint.

"Don't go that way," says Mya. "You'll get paint on your bike."

"Wait," says Tyson. "Let's make a sign to warn people about the wet paint."

"That's a good idea," says Mya.

"Let's use an apostrophe," says Mya.
"It'll let us leave out a letter and make two words into one."

"That's right!" says Tyson.
"Mrs. Lopez taught us about contractions."

"This sign should work. Now let's find the Smiths' house!" says Tyson.

"I think that's the Smiths' house," says Mya.

"No," says Tyson. "That mailbox says it's the Remmers' house."

"Why is the apostrophe after the *S*?" asks Mya.

"An apostrophe before the *S* means something belongs to one person. The apostrophe goes after the *S* here because it's the whole family's mailbox."

Remmers'

"Look," says Mya. "It's the Smiths' house!"

"That's Paul's mom and dad!" says Tyson. "There's Paul!"

"Hey guys!" says Paul. "You're just in time for a game of basketball!"

Remember to use an apostrophe:

To show when something belongs to someone:

That is Paul's bike.

To show when something belongs to more than one person:

We are going to the Smiths' house.

To join two words together to make a shorter word:

Don't go that way.